# *Oxford*
## *City Beautiful*

Credits:

*With thanks to all colleges and locations featured for their assistance and information.*

# Oxford
## *City Beautiful*

Lucy Davenport

DB PUBLISHING

First published in Great Britain in 2010 by The Derby Books
Publishing Company Limited, 3 The Parker Centre,
Derby, DE21 4SZ.

© Lucy Davenport, 2010

A catalogue record for this book is available from the British
Library.

ISBN 978-1-85983-781-8

Printed and bound by Progress Press, Malta.

# Contents

# Oxford Castle

Once home to the infamous Oxford Prison, Oxford Castle is now the site of an exciting new area of the city, containing the Malmaison Hotel, which is housed in part of the converted prison, and eight restaurants: Carluccio's, Prezzo, La Tasca, Pizza Express, Café 1071, Krispy Kreme, The Living Room and Tootsies.

Since 1071, the site of Oxford Castle has been used as a place of incarceration. This continued until 1996, when the HM Prison was closed. The historic building has been well kept and is now open to the public.

Tales of violence, executions, betrayal, romance and great escapes can all be discovered at the castle. The O3 Gallery on the site provides year-round exhibitions of the work of various artists and is definitely worth a visit.

An exciting attraction for visitors is 'Oxford Castle Unlocked', where they can learn the secrets of the castle's past.

Visitors are able to experience the severe restrictions of the 18th-century Debtors' Tower and Prison D-wing.

The castle's history features such interesting figures as Marshall William Smith, the King's prison keeper, who in the 17th century made Oxford Prison as feared and infamous as Colditz; Mary Blandy, a convicted murderess, who became an 18th-century celebrity; Jack Ketch, the public executioner and the man on whom the Punch & Judy hangman character was modelled; and Anne Green, who survived her own hanging and narrowly escaped being anatomised by an Oxford medical student in 1650.

Oxford Castle was a classic motte and bailey castle and the mound still stands today. The surviving 900-year-old underground crypt has an eerie atmosphere.

# Malmaison Hotel

Once the Victorian prison, the Malmaison has been converted into a stunning hotel. Guests even have the option of staying in one of the original cells, complete with genuine doors and bars.

The hotel rooms consist of three cells knocked together, with the original brick walls and vaulted ceilings still remaining.

The prison atrium is still intact, complete with its metal staircases and walkways, which lead to the 94 rooms spread across different wings.

Modern interior design has been sympathetically integrated into the original features of the prison, giving the hotel a distinctive feel.

The prison has featured in several television programmes and films, including a scene in the 1969 version of *The Italian Job* and TV's *Inspector Morse*. It was also used as a set for the ITV1 prison drama series, *Bad Girls*.

# County Hall

The County Hall shown here was built in 1841, although it is often mistaken for the castle as it was built in this Norman style. The County Hall is situated just in front of the castle on the roadside and houses two courtrooms, one of which is still used today. There is a tunnel underground, which leads from the old holding cells to Oxford Prison.

# Alley – Corn Exchange

Designed by H. W. Moore, the Corn Exchange was built in George Street, along with the fire station, between 1894 and 1896.

The original corn exchange was housed in the old town hall, which was demolished in 1893; however, as this meant that businesses were having to trade in the streets without any cover – far from ideal in the winter months – the Corn Exchange shown here was built.

The alley opposite the Corn Exchange has a view of Nuffield College tower. The cobbled alleys lead around the back of Cornmarket Street past various college buildings which are only accessible by foot.

Old-fashioned lanterns are used down the small paths and alleys as alternatives to lampposts.

The narrow, cobbled alleys provide shortcuts to various parts of the city. There is so much to Oxford that visitors usually miss as they keep to the main shopping streets. If you venture down these paths, however, you can discover new areas and get a real sense of adventure.

# Ashmolean Museum

The Ashmolean Museum is the first university museum in the world.

When photographed the Ashmolean was undergoing major redevelopment work. The vast project, estimated to cost £61 million, was supported by the Heritage Lottery Fund. Rick Mather is the architect behind the design for the new building work, which will affect all but the Grade I listed Cockerell building.

The Museum opened its doors on 24 May 1683 and gave the public an opportunity to see the private collection. Building work continued throughout the 20th century to make the Ashmolean what it is today.

Building work originally started in 1678 and continued for several years until 1683. The museum was initially designed to house a collection donated to the University in 1677 by Elias Ashmole.

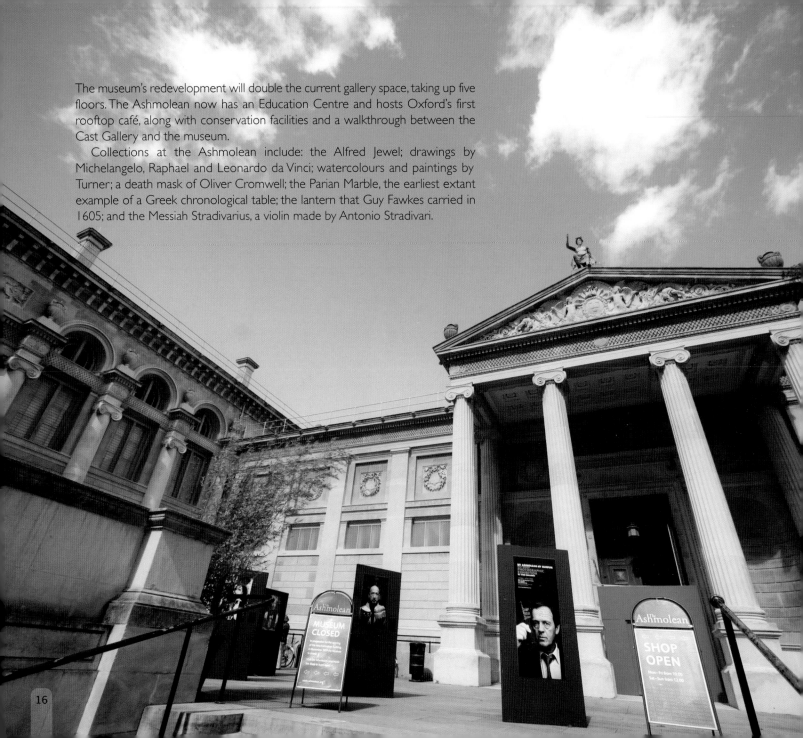

The museum's redevelopment will double the current gallery space, taking up five floors. The Ashmolean now has an Education Centre and hosts Oxford's first rooftop café, along with conservation facilities and a walkthrough between the Cast Gallery and the museum.

Collections at the Ashmolean include: the Alfred Jewel; drawings by Michelangelo, Raphael and Leonardo da Vinci; watercolours and paintings by Turner; a death mask of Oliver Cromwell; the Parian Marble, the earliest extant example of a Greek chronological table; the lantern that Guy Fawkes carried in 1605; and the Messiah Stradivarius, a violin made by Antonio Stradivari.

The outside of the theatre is decorated with 13 'Emperors' Heads', also known as the 'Caesars' or 'Apostles'. Each has a different beard or expression, but nobody knows who these heads are supposed to represent.

The Sheldonian Theatre is used for many purposes including conferences, lectures, musical recitals and various university ceremonies held throughout the year, including graduation and matriculation. In 1733 Handel performed here, giving his first recital of his third oratorio, *Athalia*. The theatre is able to seat up to 1,000 people.

# Sheldonian Theatre

The Sheldonian Theatre was designed by Sir Christopher Wren. Building work began in 1664 and took four years to complete. Described as 'one of the architectural jewels of Oxford' by the European Commission in 1994, it is still one of the top places on visitors' sight-seeing lists when in Oxford.

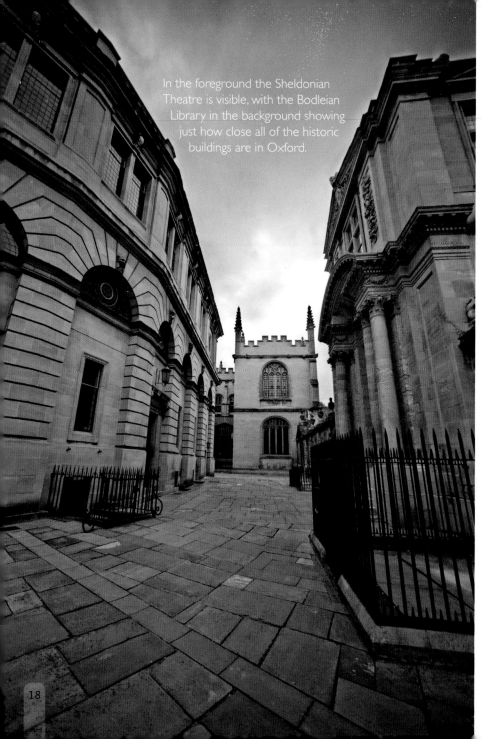

In the foreground the Sheldonian Theatre is visible, with the Bodleian Library in the background showing just how close all of the historic buildings are in Oxford.

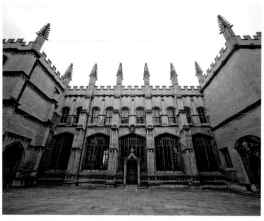

# Bodleian Library

Dating back to 1602, the Bodleian Library is one of the oldest libraries in Europe and is the University of Oxford's main library.

Thomas Bodley, a fellow at Merton College, rescued an earlier library founded in the 14th century and the new library opened in 1602 bearing his name. He died 10 years later and left money in his will to help finance the future expansion of the library.

Vast pillars lead to one entrance of the Bodleian Library. The Old School Quadrangle is situated behind this, which was completed in 1619. The tower of this is the main entrance to the library.

The library required more space in the late 18th century. The Radcliffe Camera is adjacent to the original library and was used as additional storage.

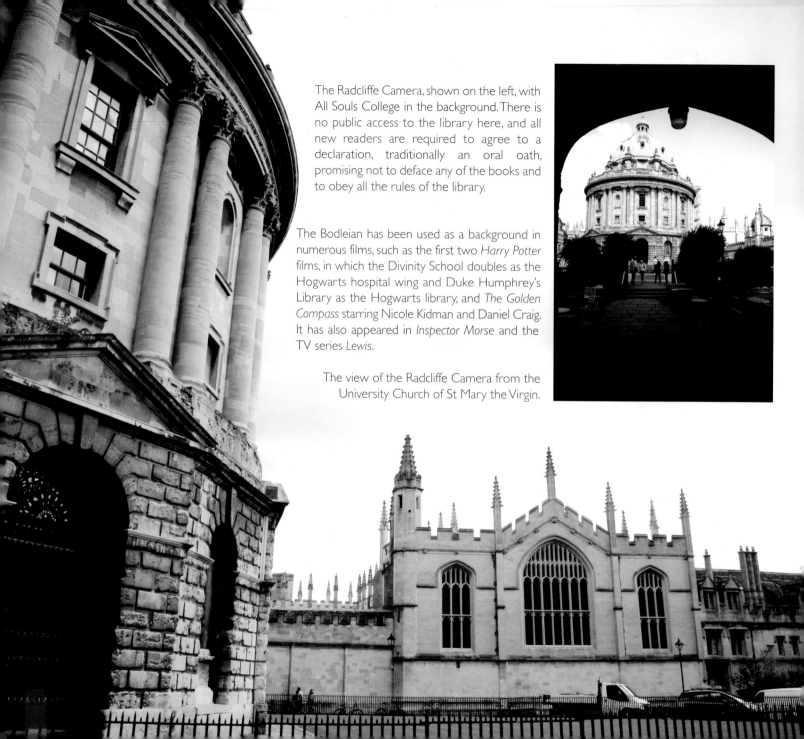

The Radcliffe Camera, shown on the left, with All Souls College in the background. There is no public access to the library here, and all new readers are required to agree to a declaration, traditionally an oral oath, promising not to deface any of the books and to obey all the rules of the library.

The Bodleian has been used as a background in numerous films, such as the first two *Harry Potter* films, in which the Divinity School doubles as the Hogwarts hospital wing and Duke Humphrey's Library as the Hogwarts library, and *The Golden Compass* starring Nicole Kidman and Daniel Craig. It has also appeared in *Inspector Morse* and the TV series *Lewis*.

The view of the Radcliffe Camera from the University Church of St Mary the Virgin.

# The University of Oxford Botanic Garden

The University of Oxford Botanic Garden is an impressive attraction all year round, not just in the spring and summer months. One of the oldest scientific gardens in the world, it is also the oldest botanic garden in Great Britain.

Founded in 1621, the Botanic Garden has been constantly updated and developed and continues to be so to this day. It is committed 'to promoting learning and glorifying nature'.

Housing several collections of plants, the garden's purposes go beyond the solely aesthetic. Plants are selected to support research and teaching programmes within the university and are a part of plant conservation projects.

The garden has a collection of over 7,000 types of plants. These are contained within three sections of the whole garden. The Glasshouses contain plants that require protection from weather elements. Outside, the Walled Garden contains the Water Garden and Rock Garden as well as the Black and Autumn Borders. Finally, the Walled Garden contains plants from different countries, families and uses.

Sir Henry Danvers donated £5,000 in order to set up a physic garden. The site used was on the River Cherwell in an area belonging to Magdalen College. The walls and arches were finished in 1633 and by their completion all of the money had been spent, which left nothing to pay for the running of the garden.

A footpath within the main garden leading over a bridge, surrounded by autumn plants.

The Danby gateway leading to the Botanic Garden is one of the three entrances that were designed by Nicholas Stone.

The Botanic Garden has been a place of inspiration for many people. It was frequently visited by Lewis Carroll in the 1860s as inspiration for *Alice's Adventures in Wonderland*. Sir John Tenniel's illustration of the Queen's Croquet-Ground shows the garden's water lily house in the background. J.R.R. Tolkien often spent time in the gardens as well.

The view of Magdalen College from the Botanic Gardens.

# Punting boats

Punting in Oxford is a quiet and relaxing way to experience the city. Most of the punting is done on the River Cherwell, which takes you under Magdalen Bridge.

The tradition in Oxford is to punt from inside the boat, as opposed from on top of the till. The boat is positioned with the till end at the front, and this technique dates back to 1880.

Punting in Oxford is part of a long tradition in the city, along with rowing. Crews can often be seen being put through their paces in preparation for the regattas.

# Saïd Business School

Saïd Business School was established in 1996 and is a part of Oxford University. It has a strong reputation across Europe as one of the best entrepreneurial business schools.

The building was designed by Dixon and Jones, who were also the architects behind the Royal Opera House in London.

An extension of the school has been planned for the near future, with a new building costing an estimated £25 million at the centre of the design. This will provide the additional facilities the school requires. This photograph shows the front of the school, where the school's library is visible to passers-by. Glass fronted, the two-floor Sainsbury Library is quite a sight, especially at night.

The school provides some of the most modern architecture to be seen in Oxford. The design is incredible and all aspects have been carefully considered. There are even further surprises inside which are not visible from the road. These include a classical outdoor amphitheatre, columns and cloisters.

# Nuffield College

Designed by Austen Harrison, the plans for Nuffield College were approved in 1940, although the college was not built until the mid-1950s.

The land for the college was donated by William Morris, 1st Viscount Nuffield. It was previously the city's main canal basin.

This sculpture *Fountain* was created by Hubert Dalwood as a commission for Nuffield College in 1962, and was selected by Henry Moore. Dalwood was a British abstract sculptor who broke away from the conventions of the 1950s.

Wall sculpture near the porters lodge.

The stone tower, visible here with a steel spire, houses the college library. The college specialises in the social sciences, particularly economics, politics and sociology.

# St Anne's College

St Anne's College was the result of a coalition in the Victorian years between women and men who believed that women should be allowed to study at Oxford University.

St Anne's College is located between the main Banbury and Woodstock Roads, just outside the centre of Oxford. The college buildings are within a five-acre area.

A large wooden door at St Anne's College with stone decoration above.

Founded in 1879, it was originally called The Society of Home-Students. It allowed women to study there and live in lodgings around the city. In 1952 the college became an established part of the university.

# St Cross College

St Cross College was established together with Iffley (now Wolfson) College, due to pressures on the university, during the early 1960s.

Looking through an arch to the quad of St Cross College. The college was set up in 1965 by the university, with its first graduate students being admitted the following year.

The original location of St Cross was on St Cross Road, but it moved to St Giles in 1981. The old site on St Cross Road was made into the Islamic Studies Centre. In 1996 St Cross College and Brasenose College completed the building of two residential structures.

Pusey House buildings were designed by the architects Temple and Leslie Moore.

The arches lead to a second quadrangle. This enabled further extension for the college, which opened in 1993.

The 'Four Arches Arch', which can be found behind the main buildings. This was named after the four colleges, Christ Church, All Souls, St John's and Merton.

# St Edmund Hall

In 1957 St Edmund Hall officially became a college; however, its history dates back to the 13th century.

The college coat of arms can be found above the entrance to the Porters' Lodge. The arms show a red cross with four Cornish Choughs.

This bronze sculpture shows St Edmund reading. It was unveiled in 2007 in the grounds of St Edmund Hall and was created by Rodney Munday.

The college was named after St Edmund of Abingdon. This photograph shows the front quadrangle, parts of which date back to the late 16th century.

The Old Library,
photographed here, dates
from the late 17th century.
Access to this can only be
granted during university
vacations and after a written
application. It houses the
works of Tomas Hearne and
John Oldham.

The dining hall at St Edmund Hall has a spectacular ceiling. It is made up of arches and wooden panels, with what look like white handkerchiefs uplit by LED lights. The colours change, and the light can be controlled to give different levels for day and evening dining.

This is St Peter-in-the-East, a 12th-century church which is situated in the grounds of St Edmund Hall. This now houses the college library, with the ancient churchyard, lawns and trees still surrounding.

The view of St Peter's and St Edmund Hall from the road. The church was built in around 1140 by Robert D'Oilly. The exterior of the church has stone borders and still features several old stained-glass windows, some of which date back to the 13th century.

# New College

Do not be fooled by the name, as New College in Oxford is actually over 620 years old. Founded in 1379, its official name is also that of Oriel College – the College of St Mary. As a result, this was called 'the new College of St Mary'.

The grand archway leading into the college grounds. The Holywell Street entrance was regarded as the back entrance to the college in 1772, as it lay outside the city wall.

A stone, spiral staircase within New College.

New College was the first college to be designed around a quadrangle plan. The college was founded at the end of the 14th century by William of Wykeham, Bishop of Winchester.

The dramatic wooden-panelled corridor leading to the dining hall.

The dining hall ready for the lunchtime sitting.

A view of the bell tower, which has one of the oldest rings of 10 bells, and the chapel pinnacles.

The millennium sundial at New College. The dial is 17ft tall and is carved into the Muniment Tower. 'MM' is visible at the top of the sundial to represent the millennium (2000), and this is inverted at the bottom as 'WW', which stands for William of Wyckham.

A stone sculpture found on the wall at New College.

The main quad of New College. Across the quad is the Queens Lane entrance. The chapel is visible on the right of the photograph.

The interior of New College chapel looking towards the altar. People to have graduated from New College include Hugh Grant, Kate Beckinsale and politicians Tony Benn and Michael Meacher.

The original stained-glass windows were designed by Sir Joshua Reynolds in the 18th century, but many of them have since had to be restored. The choir stalls shown here have 62 misericords. These are wooden shelves located underneath the folding seats of the stalls. They were copied for use at Canterbury Cathedral in Victorian times.

The gate leading to the mound in the gardens.
The beautiful gardens are a delight to walk
around, and the mound is a common
decorative feature of Tudor gardens.

A part of the city wall stands in the
grounds of New College. William of
Wykeham entered into an agreement
when he founded the college that he
would maintain the City Wall. This
arrangement is still upheld today, with an
inspection scheduled every three years.

# Jesus College

Jesus College is the only Oxford College to date from the reign of Queen Elizabeth I. Located right in the heart of Oxford, Jesus College is situated between Turl Street and Market Street, with the majority of the buildings dating from the 17th century, including the Front and Second Quadrangles.

The Front Quad entrance, showing the chapel on the right. The Victorian chapel was extended in 1636.

The limestone used in the building suffers greatly from airborne pollution and damp weather conditions. As a result, large areas of the college have had to be refaced. Some of the earlier Headington stone still remains, however.

The view across the immaculate lawns in the quad. The old and new stone colours are visible on the far buildings.

# Keble College

Keble College first accepted students in 1870. The college was founded in memory of John Keble, who was a member of the 'Tractarian' movement.

The library has beautiful stained-glass windows, raised bays and patterned brickwork throughout. In 1981 the library was extended with reading rooms on the ground floor, which can be accessed from the main library area.

The Victorian reading room was designed by William Butterfield and opened in 1878.

The grand dining hall.

An impressive window seat in the area between the dining hall and the library.

The patterned brickwork is continued throughout the college, both inside and out.

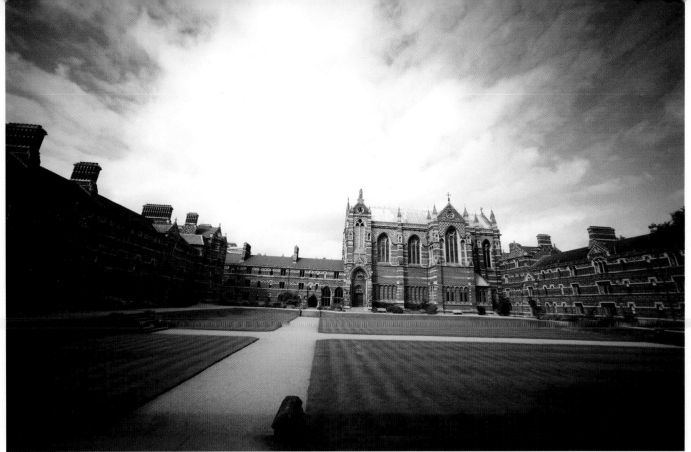

John Keble had a profound impact on the Church of England during the mid-19th century, which made Keble College stand out.

The view of the college chapel across the quad through the arches.

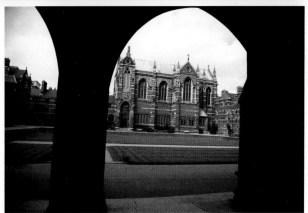

An old bell found in the college grounds.

Small details on the walls include painted names.

The college victories and crests are chalked onto the walls outside the halls of residence.

The grand doors leading from the quad to the chapel, which was opened on St Mark's Day in 1876.

The architect of the chapel was William Butterfield. It is spectacular inside featuring patterned brickwork, pillars, high ceilings and stained-glass windows.

# University Parks

The vast University Parks are located on the River Cherwell. The park is about 70 acres (30 hectares) on the west bank, with a further four acres (1.5 hectares) towards the south. Traditionally referred to as Mesopotamia, this is situated amid the upper and lower levels of the river.

Over an 11-year period from 1853, a total of 91 acres (37 hectares) of land was purchased for the Parks by the University from Merton College. From this land, four acres (1.5 hectares) were allocated to be used for the University Museum. The museum was completed in 1860. A further area was taken over between 1912 and the early 1950s for buildings in the University Science Area.

The university was presented with a plan for the parks in June 1863 by Mr James Bateman of Magdalen College. This was rejected, however, and in 1865 the university allotted £500 to go towards purchasing trees and shrubs.

The initial plantings were carried out under the supervision of Mr William Baxter, then the Superintendent of the University Botanic Garden, and directed by the Revd Thomas Hopkins, curator.

Further tree planting was carried out in 1888, the 1920s and in the 1950s after many of the exotic trees previously planted did not survive. In more recent years, starting in 1977, many saplings have been planted. These have had little impression on the landscape at the present time but will ensure that future generations and visitors will have enjoyment when visiting the park.

University Sports makes good use of the parks in day-to-day life. This is overseen by the Committee for Sport and is separate from the Park Curators. Home to Oxford University Cricket Club since 1881, the park's cricket ground is considered to be one of the most attractive in the country. The pavilion in the park was designed by Sir Thomas Jackson and has been sited the same distance from the wicket as the pavilion at Lord's.

Bateman's original design actually included a two-and-a-half-acre ornamental water; however, a pond was not constructed in the parks until 1925. The pond was originally circular and dug out by hand. It was extended in size in early 1996 so that it is now more in keeping with the rest of the park. It more closely resembles the water included in the park's original plans.

Since the pond's redevelopment there has been better access to the water for children to feed the ducks, and it now provides perfect conditions for plants requiring moisture. Plants throughout the parks have been chosen to provide flowers throughout the year, with shape, texture and colours also taken into consideration in order to keep the views spectacular, whatever the time of year.

# Hertford College

Hart Hall on Catte Street was founded in the 13th century by Elias de Hertford, and the oldest parts of the college are still situated there, including the Old Hall and the Old Quadrangle.

During the 18th century Hart Hall was rejected in the Principal's application to be accepted as a full college of the University, and the site was taken over by Magdalen Hall. Sir Thomas Baring was a huge supporter of the college's cause, and in 1874 the college was established as Hertford College by an Act of Parliament, thanks largely to Baring's benefaction.

One of the tower buildings at Hertford College.

The view across the quad through the archway.

Jackson was also behind the building of this chapel, which is on the south side of the Old Quadrangle.

Sir Thomas Jackson designed the hall, and the spiral stonework seen here houses the staircase.

The view out of the slanted windows of the spiral tower out over the quad.

# Brasenose Lane

Brasenose Lane is located between Radcliffe Square and Turl Street in the centre of Oxford.

The lane links Exeter College, Lincoln College and Brasenose College, with high stone buildings on each side.

Brasenose Lane is used as an unofficial cycle path by students. Before women were allowed into the university it was known as the common 'meeting place'.

A door leading inside Brasenose College.

# Brasenose College

Brasenose College was originally the site of Brasenose Hall, an institution which started out as lodging houses before it was turned into a place of learning.

Brasenose College records state the year of foundation as 1509, as this was when a quarry in Headington provided the stone for the new buildings. The college was to be called 'The King's Hall and College of Brasenose'.

Brasenose College was founded by Sir Richard Sutton, a lawyer, and William Smyth, the Bishop of Lincoln. The college has kept strong links with Cheshire and Lancashire as both founders were from the North-West. Smyth provided the funding for the building and Sutton obtained the site.

Originally the college consisted of one quadrangle with the tower standing very grandly over the site. At the time the college was only two storeys high, so it would have looked quite different before the Radcliffe Camera was constructed.

In the 17th century the college began to require more space, and their solution was to build a third storey, which is how it stands today. The work took 20 years to complete and was started in 1614.

The view over the quadrangle with the Tower of Brasenose also visible. Beyond this is the Radcliffe Camera and, to the right, the University Church of St Mary the Virgin.

The sundial is a main feature in the quadrangle. Past students of Brasenose College include David Cameron and Michael Palin.

The chalking on the walls is common within each college to show sporting victories. The one shown here is from 2008 in Brasenose College for the women's First and Second VIIIs (rowing).

The College Chapel was built at the same time as the library, between 1655 and 1666. John Jackson oversaw the building of these areas and was paid £1 per week to do so.

# All Souls College

All Souls College was the sole responsibility of Henry Chichele, Archbishop of Canterbury. It was planned, built and endowed in the 1430s.

During the time of foundation, Chichele was in his 70s and this was his third Oxford benefaction. In 1438 King Henry VI granted All Souls College its foundation charter.

Chichele secured the site for the college on the corner of the High Street and Catte Street. It is immediately next to St Mary the Virgin Church, which is visible over the college buildings here.

The detailed stone fan-vaulted passageway leading to the chapel.

The corridor leading to the College Chapel. Inside the chapel there are statues of saints, bishops and monarchs.

The baroque chapel screen was designed by Sir James Thornhill in 1716. It replaced a screen that was attributed to Christopher Wren.

The corridor leading to the College Chapel. Inside the chapel there are statues of saints, bishops and monarchs.

All Souls from the Gate Tower, which leads from the Radcliffe
Camera into All Souls North Quad.

The towers of the North Quad.

The Great Hall and sundial, which
was designed by Christopher
Wren. It was positioned here in
Victorian times, but initially, in the
18th century, it was located
between the south-facing
pinnacles of the chapel.

# Christ Church College

Originally founded in 1524 by Cardinal Wolsey as Cardinal's College, Christ Church is one of the largest colleges in Oxford.

Christ Church has produced 13 Prime Ministers and has had many influential students including John Locke, John Wesley and Lewis Carroll, as well as several Cabinet ministers, bishops and civil servants. Many of the scenes in the *Harry Potter* films were shot at Christ Church College. The Great Hall was replicated in film studios to create Hogwarts Hall.

# Pembroke College

Pembroke College was founded in 1624. Fellows of the college include J.R.R. Tolkien and Senator J. William Fulbright. There have also been several notable scientists who have studied and worked there through the centuries, as well as theologians and lawyers, including John Moore, who went on to become the Archbishop of Canterbury in 1783.

Masters of Pembroke College include the neurologist and record-breaking runner, Sir Roger Bannister. The photograph here shows the area in the gallery of the dining hall where Bannister's memorabilia is on show. Exhibits cover his athletic and academic careers.

The chapel at Pembroke College was constructed between 1728 and 1732. William Townsend designed and built the chapel, as prior to this students had to worship in the Docklinton aisle of St Aldate's Church. The painting over the altar in the distance of the photograph is copied from Rubens' painting in Antwerp and was added to the chapel in 1786. Then, in 1884, graduate of the college Charles Kempe was asked to redesign the interior. In 1893 an organ was added to the chapel after a petition from the students, and this was built by Charles Martin and lasted for 100 years before a replacement was required. This was made by a Canadian organ builder, Fernand Létourneau, and was his first creation in England. The College Chapel has since gone through restoration work on both the interior and exterior due to pollution. This was aided generously by Dr Damon Wells, an American alumnus.

A photograph of the dining hall taken from the gallery above. It is a stunning hall with stained-glass windows throughout and a black vaulted ceiling.

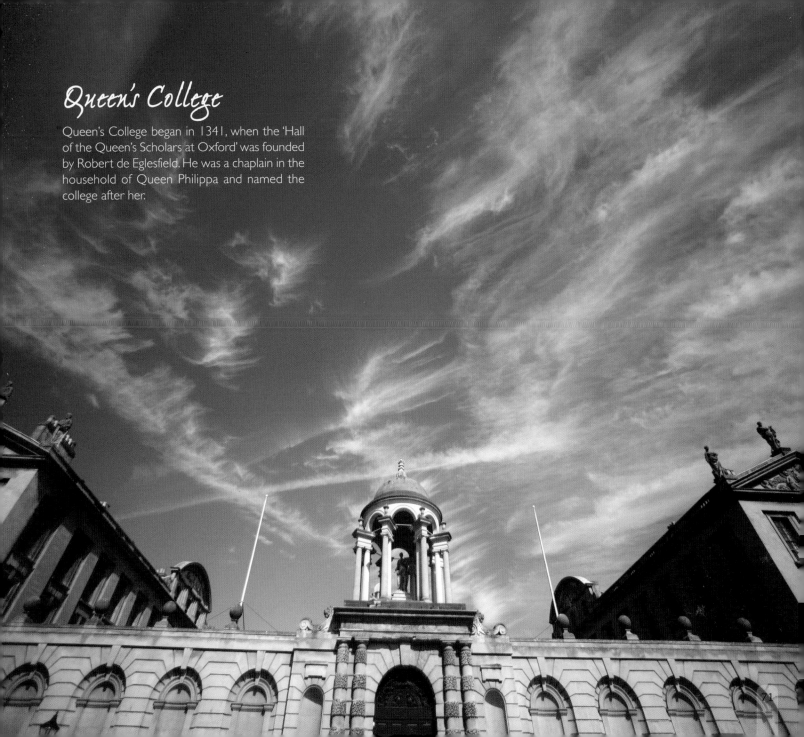

# Queen's College

Queen's College began in 1341, when the 'Hall of the Queen's Scholars at Oxford' was founded by Robert de Eglesfield. He was a chaplain in the household of Queen Philippa and named the college after her.

# Magdalen College

Magdalen College was founded in 1458 on the site of the Hospital of St John by William Waynflete, Bishop of Winchester and Lord Chancellor; however, work did not commence until 1467 due to political disputes. When the building work began, they started initially on Longwall and then moved onto the main Cloister Quadrangle in 1474. This was then followed by the library, hall and chapel. Famous alumni include Oscar Wilde and King Edward VIII.

May Morning traditions dating back over 500 years start early at 6am on May Day, with the Magdalen College Choir singing *Hymnus Eucharisticus* from the top of Magdalen tower. Large crowds gather on Magdalen Bridge and the High Street and there is a real party atmosphere, normally following all-night balls held the night before.

# Merton Street

St John Street became known as Merton Street in the 19th century, and by the 20th century the whole of the L-shaped road had become known as Merton Street. The part of the street around the corner that runs parallel with the High Street still has its original cobbles, which date from the 18th century onwards, and the road surface is Grade II listed. Merton College, Oxford's second-oldest college, is situated to the south of the street. To the west of Merton, Corpus Christi College, one of Oxford's smallest colleges, also fronts onto the street. At the western end, actually in Oriel Square, is the entrance to Christ Church, Oxford's largest college.

# Merton College

Merton College was founded in 1264 by Walter de Merton. The hall and the chapel and the rest of the front quad were complete before the end of the 13th century. Well-known Mertonians include J.R.R. Tolkien, Sir Andrew Wiles and Sir Thomas Bodley.

A student's bicycle outside the entrance to Merton College.

# Corpus Christi College

Corpus Christi College was founded by Richard Fox, Bishop of Winchester, in 1517. Bishop Fox had initially intended the college for the training of monks.

One of the Corpus Christi College buildings on Merton Street.

# University College

Originally University College was only open to Fellows reading Theology, but in the early 16th century, when the majority of the other colleges started to accept undergraduates, University College followed.

As University grew in size work began in 1634 to replace the original mediaeval buildings with a new Front Quad. Although half of the new quad was completed by 1640, being paid for by former college members, the other half took almost 30 years to complete due to the Civil War. The other main quadrangle, Radcliffe Quad, took only three years to build in 1716–19 and was financed by a former member, John Radcliffe, whose statue is located there.

# Somerville College

Founded as Somerville Hall in 1879, the college's mission was to provide an opportunity for women, who at that date were excluded from the university, allowing them to enter higher education within Oxford. The decision to abolish religious tests for the students set the standards that the college follows to this day.

The college was named after Mary Somerville, an accomplished early female mathematician.

The arches of
Somerville College.

Looking from the lodge's entrance into the quad.

# Wolfson College

The university founded Iffley College in 1965. It was renamed Wolfson College and admitted its first students in October 1968.

The path leading to the gardens of the college.

Wolfson College is visible down the driveway.

College buildings in the River Quad.

The college buildings were designed by architects Powell and Moya and were ready in 1974. The college received its Royal Charter in 1981. These are views of the River Quad.

Images of the punting boats, which you can hire just next to the college at Cherwell Boathouse.

The harbour at the college.

# Wycliffe Hall

Wycliffe Hall was founded in 1877 by a group of churchmen.

The view from the gardens to the back of Wycliffe Hall.

A crest carved out of stone, which is positioned within the walls of the college.

A detail of the sign for Wycliffe Hall.

A series of the doors found around the buildings.

The brickwork and masonry of the tower.

The repetition shown within the windows of Wycliffe Hall.

# Kellogg College

Kellogg College is Oxford's 36th college. The college was founded on 1 March 1990 (as Rewley House) and was named in honour of Mr W.K. Kellogg on 1 October 1994. This was in recognition of the generous support given by the W.K. Kellogg Foundation to the university over the years.

An atmospheric shot of the chimneys.

Two doors within the college grounds sporting the blue colour scheme.

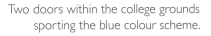

The college sign with the building in the background.

The exterior of the college showing the detailing of the building, especially the roof.

The gardens and the back of the college.

# Lady Margaret Hall

The entrance to Lady Margaret Hall, which was founded in 1878 by Edward Talbot. In 1978, 100 years after its foundation, Lady Margaret Hall accepted women.

The main quad area of Lady Margaret Hall.

The crest of Lady Margaret Hall in stone on the wall.

The pillars leading out into the quad.

A statue figure in the walls of the hall.

A gateway leading to another aspect of the college.

The back of Lady Margaret Hall, seen from the gardens.

An alley leading from Lady Margaret Hall to the University Parks.

Lady Margaret Hall is named in honour of Lady Margaret Beaufort.

# The University Church of St Mary the Virgin

In the centre of Oxford, the University Church of St Mary the Virgin stands in the centre of the old walled city, with the university buildings having been built around it.

The front of the church, taken from the High Street entrance.

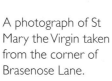

A photograph of St Mary the Virgin taken from the corner of Brasenose Lane.

The view from the gallery down to the altar.

St Mary's remains the formal place of worship for the university.

Latimer, Ridley and Cranmer, the three Anglican bishops who were burnt at the stake in Oxford, underwent part of their trial in St Mary's. First tried in April 1554, Ridley and Latimer underwent the ordeal again in 1555.

Here is the immense stained-glass window at the rear of the church in the gallery.

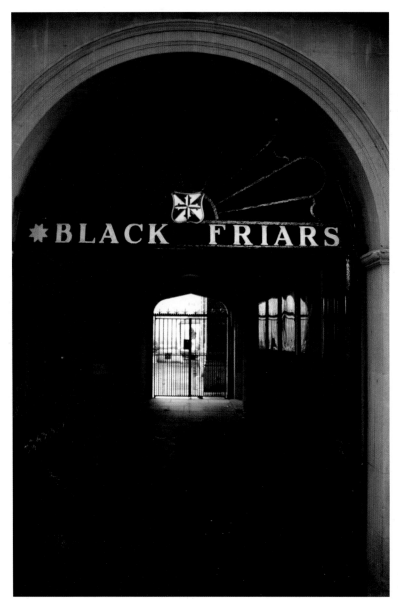

The view towards the back of the chapel showing the beautiful stonework of the gallery area and the two vast windows either side.

# Blackfriars Hall

Established on 1 January 1994, Blackfriars Hall is a Permanent Private Hall of the University of Oxford. It is run by English Dominicans living a common life of prayer, study and preaching.

The friars are known as Dominicans after St Dominic, the founder of the order. In the Middle Ages they were known as Black Friars after their cloaks, or black 'cappas', which they still wear over their white habits.

Members of Blackfriars Hall read both undergraduate and postgraduate degrees. These are normally within the fields of philosophy and theology, although English literature, British history and classics can be studied by visiting students.

The large window at the front of the chapel.

A plaque on the wall of the chapel.

The stone, spiralling staircase is a feature of Blackfriars Hall.

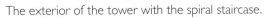

The detailed ceiling of the dining hall.

The exterior of the tower with the spiral staircase.

The inside of the chapel has an arched ceiling.

## St Michael's at the North Gate

St Michael's at the North Gate is an 11th-century building, the only one remaining in Oxford.

The view of the church from the first floor. In this area there is a display of rare silver dating from 1562.

The stained-glass windows of the church, with the gallery of the first floor to the left.

On the way up the tower visitors will pass several displays, including these church bells, along with the door to the martyrs' prison cell.

The glass front to the gift shop and entrance of St Michael's, which has been added in recent years.

The view from the top of the tower. It is hard to believe that the Saxon architecture once formed part of the city wall and was faced by rolling countryside.

The church buildings have evolved over several centuries, starting in the 13th century with the sanctuary and the south aisle, moving onto the lady chapel and organ transept in the 14th century and finally the north aisle in the 15th century.

The actual church and tower have remained unchanged since the 15th century, having only undergone improvements. The tower was restored in 1986.

# Town Hall

Since 1292 a Guild Hall had stood on this site, but this was replaced by the Town Hall in 1752, the Guild Hall eventually being demolished in 1893. The site is now the new Municipal Building, which houses the council offices, court, police station and public library, but the whole site has become known as the Town Hall.

The grand stairs leading up from the ground-floor reception area.

The area at the top of the stairs which leads to the Main Hall has several display cabinets on show.

The Main Hall is 90ft long, and the stage can hold around 200 performers in its tiers. There are dressing rooms available for performers under the stage. The organ featured behind the stage was made by Henry Willis and Son in 1896–97, and it is still in its original condition.

The Main Hall covers the old Corn Exchange. This photograph shows the galleries that cover the sides in the hall.

Paintings housed in the assembly room.

# Turl Street

Exeter, Jesus and Lincoln College are all located on Turl Street, which has been pedestrianised since 1985. In 1363 it was originally called St Mildred's Street and in the mid-17th century became known as Turl Gate Street. This name derived from a twirling gate, which was demolished in 1722.

# Bridge of Sighs

Hertford Bridge is best known as the Bridge of Sighs. Crossing over New College Lane, the covered bridge is referred to as the Bridge of Sighs due to its similarity to the one in Venice; however, it actually bears more resemblance to the Rialto Bridge.

In fact, the bridge was not intended to be a replica of its Venetian counterpart and was designed by Sir Thomas Jackson in 1914. It links the Old and New Quadrangles of Hertford College and was originally objected to by New College.

# Covered Market

The Covered Market is a historic market place with permanent stalls, with entrances on the High Street and Market Street. Still thriving today, the Covered Market officially opened on 1 November 1774. The market was established to clear up the untidy stalls from the main streets of central Oxford.

John Gwynn, the architect behind Magdalen Bridge, planned and created the ideas for the market's High Street front with the four entrances. In 1772 a market committee was formed; half of the members came from the university, and half from the town. They accepted an estimate for the building of 20 butchers' shops of just over £916.

Twenty more stalls soon followed and after 1773 meat was allowed to be sold only inside the market. The market grew, with stalls being set up for dairy products, fish, pork and garden produce. Today the market is home to stalls of all trades. Traditional shops sell fresh produce, as well as modern-day additions such as gift and clothing shops.

# Doors

A selection of beautiful doorways in Oxford city centre.

# Gormley Statue

Antony Gormley, the sculptor who was also behind the *Angel of the North*, was commissioned by Exeter College to create a statue of a nude man. This has been placed on the roof of Blackwell's Art and Poster shop on the corner of Broad and Turl Street. Unveiled in February 2009, the commission was paid for by an anonymous benefactor. The statue is part of a series called 'Another Time II'. Gormley read history of art at Trinity College and visited Exeter College during the chapel restoration work to express an interest in producing a stone statue for the site.

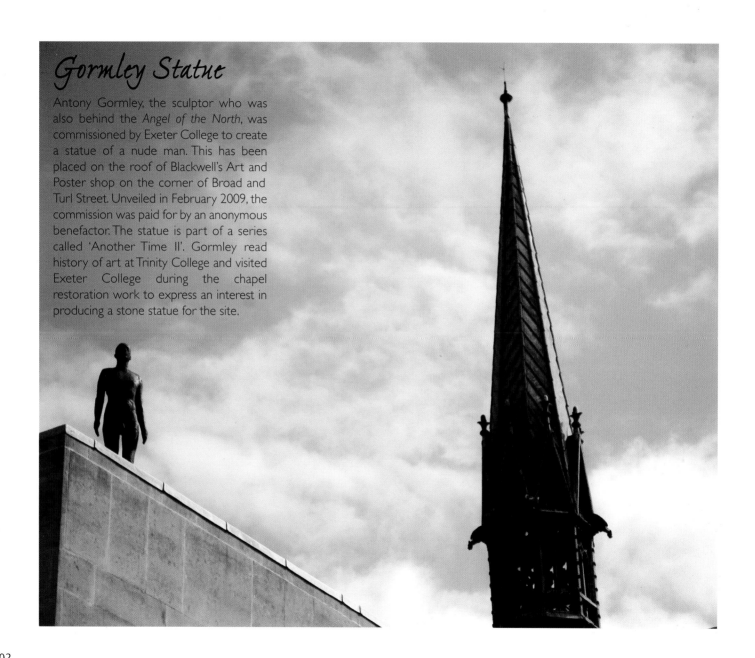

# Alice's Shop

Alice's shop can be found just across from Christ Church College. The shop itself was written into the Alice adventures over 140 years ago and is one of the most genuine links to an entire story in the *Alice in Wonderland* adventures.

In the 1850s Lewis Carroll wrote a story for Alice Liddell, the daughter of the Dean of Christ Church College,

which was also illustrated by him. Carroll was encouraged to publish his work, which was an instant success and is now known worldwide.

Carroll often used real scenes and characters that were familiar to Alice Liddell so she could relate to them.

ALICE'S SHOP

Alice's Shop contains a fantastic array of collectables and certainly warrants a visit by both children and adults.

The book of *Alice's Adventures in Wonderland*.

A variety of key chains for sale in the shop.

Alice decorations.

Everything is Alice related; for example, here is Mad Hatter Tea presented in a hat!

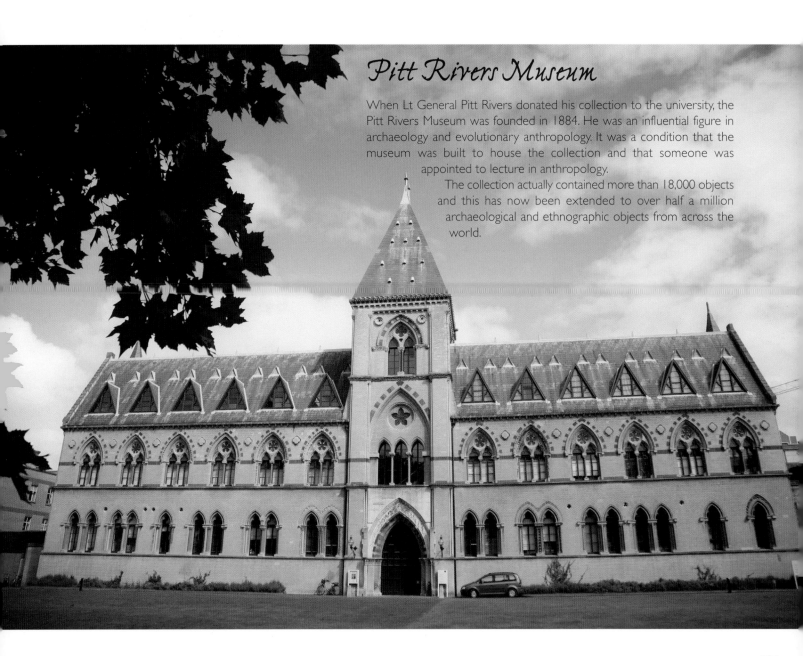

# Pitt Rivers Museum

When Lt General Pitt Rivers donated his collection to the university, the Pitt Rivers Museum was founded in 1884. He was an influential figure in archaeology and evolutionary anthropology. It was a condition that the museum was built to house the collection and that someone was appointed to lecture in anthropology.

The collection actually contained more than 18,000 objects and this has now been extended to over half a million archaeological and ethnographic objects from across the world.

# Museum of the History of Science

The entrance to the Museum of the History of Science. Located on Broad Street, it houses an impressive collection of scientific instruments and is the world's oldest surviving purpose-built museum building. The construction itself was completed in 1683.

One of the rooms of exhibits containing several glass cabinets and displays.

The dark wooden stairs with a chandelier hanging down the centre.

The stained-glass windows on the stairs inside the museum.

The museum is a department of the University of Oxford. Not only is the museum open to the public, but it is also available for study by those who want to go beyond the library books.

The doorway leading from the stairs through to the entrance area.

The grand display units.

There are approximately 10,000 objects within the museum. These cover all areas of the history of science, from old antiques through to the present day.

The view from the top of the stairs at the entrance to the museum looking out onto Broad Street.

Collections include astrolabes, sundials, quadrants, mathematical instruments, microscopes, telescopes and old cameras, and include the chemistry apparatus shown here.

# Carfax Tower

St Martin's Church and tower was rebuilt in 1818; however, due to traffic problems the road required widening at the end of the 19th century and the church was demolished in 1896. The two 'quarter boys' can be seen here on the east with the church clock. These were recast from the originals by Richard Keene.

The tower stands 74ft tall, and the name 'Carfax' derives from the French 'carrefour', meaning 'crossroads'.

Climbing the 99 steps to the top of the Carfax Tower, you get a bird's-eye view of Oxford's 'dreaming spires'.

The view down the High Street with St Mary the Virgin and the Radcliffe Camera visible in the distance.

The sights of Christ Church College.

Roof tops, the dreaming spires of All Souls College and the Radcliffe Camera.

# The Plain

The Plain was made into a roundabout in 1950 and is located east of Magdalen Bridge, leading to St Clement's, Iffley Road and Cowley Road. The Plain was given its name after St Clement's Church was demolished in 1828.

The plaque shown here in the pavement outlines the history of the Plain. The Plain houses the Victorian Fountain, which was designed by E.P. Warren. Built in 1899, it is supported by stone columns and has a roof with a clock at the top.

# Tolkien Door

Born in England, John Ronald Reuel Tolkien was a writer, poet, philologist and university professor. He is best known for his high fantasy books such as *The Hobbit*, *The Lord of the Rings* and *The Silmarillion*. He was a close friend of C.S. Lewis and they were both members of the Inklings, an informal literary discussion group. No. 21 Merton Street, photographed here, was Tolkien's home from 1971–73.

# St Aldate's Church

St Aldate's dates back to Saxon times. Its first major constructions date from the 12th century, along with the central strand of the building as it stands today. The church has since been extended and remodelled at various times.

The original tower was built in the 13th century and was rebuilt in its entirety in 1873.

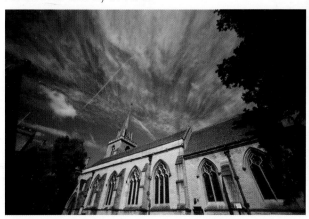

# Maison Blanc

Raymond Blanc is one of the world's most respected chefs and his skills are totally self-taught. In 1977 Raymond and his wife Jenny opened their first restaurant, which was located in Oxford and called Les Quat'Saisons. This was an overnight success and Blanc was awarded Egon Ronay Restaurant of the Year and Michelin stars, among other awards.

In July 2009, Raymond Blanc was awarded the Lifetime Achievement Award at the 2009 Catey Awards.

There are now 15 Maison Blanc stores in the south of England, with sites including London, Henley-on-Thames, Guildford and Winchester.

Since this time Raymond Blanc has embarked on other projects, including the prestigious Le Manoir aux Quat'Saisons in Great Milton, Oxford. This is the only country house hotel in the UK which has been awarded two Michelin Stars for a total of 19 years.

In December 2008, Raymond Blanc undertook a major relaunch of the brand Maison Blanc. The store here in Oxford was the original store, selling a vast selection of breads and cakes.

# Quod

Quod is located on Oxford's High Street. The Quod Brasserie forms part of the Old Bank Hotel. Originally a banking hall, the transformation was designed by Jeremy Mogford and has since become a very successful restaurant.

Inside, Quod is very contemporary and stylish and has a great feeling of space.

The outside terrace, located at the rear of Quod, is perfect for the summer months and escaping the busy High Street.

Quod houses an impressive collection of art by young British artists on the walls within the restaurant.

The Old Bank, located next door to Quod, was originally Barclays bank. The building dates from the 18th century, with its present state dating from 2000. It is an incredible setting and location.

Quod is also part of Gee's Restaurant, the Old Parsonage and, as mentioned, the Old Bank.

# Jamie's Italian

Jamie's Italian in Oxford was the first of its kind. It was created by chef Jamie Oliver to present an accessible and affordable place to eat where everyone is welcome.

Never shy of a challenge, the success of Jamie's Italian is due to his hard work and incredible team. The Oxford restaurant has since been extended and has proved very popular. There have also been six other such restaurants opened in the UK.

Jamie Oliver wanted to re-create what Italians are most proud of – and he has done just that!

This photograph shows one part of the restaurant, which also extends to the left as well as downstairs.

The restaurant uses local and Italian seasonal produce. Even walking past the restaurant before it opens you will see the chefs carefully rolling the fresh pasta.

Jamie Oliver's cookbooks on sale.

## Bikes

Oxford city centre is best visited on foot or, like many locals, by bicycle. Oxford was the site of the first Park-and-Ride system in the country. It opened in 1973 with space for 250 cars.

# St Giles' Fair

St Giles' Fair has been held on the Monday and Tuesday following the first Sunday after St Giles' Day (1 September) since the 19th century. In the early 17th century, the fair evolved from the St Giles' parish wake, and this later became recognised as St Giles' Feast.

The city corporation, now the City Council, took over the control of the fair in 1930. The area is closed to traffic for two days each year when the traditional fair takes place.

The University Parks are also closed during this time to show that they are owned by the University of Oxford as opposed to being public.

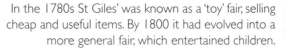

Amusements for adults were introduced from the 1830s. There were numerous calls to close the fair at the end of the 19th century, however, due to complaints of rowdiness.

In the 1780s St Giles' was known as a 'toy' fair, selling cheap and useful items. By 1800 it had evolved into a more general fair, which entertained children.

# Broad Street

Broad Street is famous for its bookshops, including the original Blackwell's bookshop. Balliol College, Trinity College and Exeter College are located on this street, as well as the Museum of the History of Science, Sheldonian Theatre and the new Bodleian Library building.

# Street Entertainer

A street entertainer on Cornmarket Street.

# St Mary's Passage

St Mary's Passage was built in 1887 and runs between the new quadrangle of Brasenose College and the University Church of St Mary the Virgin. It leads to Radcliffe Square and is referred to as Radcliffe Street on some 19th-century maps.

# Dreaming Spires

Oxford is known as the 'city of dreaming spires', a term coined by poet Matthew Arnold in reference to the harmonious architecture of Oxford's university buildings. Arnold won an open scholarship to Balliol College in 1841.

# St Mary Magdalen

This is St Mary Magdalen Church in the centre of Oxford. A wooden church, dedicated to St Mary Magdalen, stood on this site a thousand years ago, although it was then outside the northern wall of the city. When the Viking raiders burnt down much of Oxford in 1010 and 1013, the wooden church appears to have been lost.

In 1074, Robert D'Oilly, the Norman Constable of Oxford, built a single-aisled chapel to replace the Saxon foundation. St Hugh, Bishop of Lincoln, rebuilt the church in 1194, during the reign of Richard I.

# Cornmarket Street

Cornmarket Street is one of the main shopping streets in the centre of Oxford. Fully pedestrianised, it leads from St Giles to the Carfax Tower and the High Street. Boswells of Oxford is one of the long-standing stores on this street and has been trading on Cornmarket Street since 1738. In 1928 it expanded, moving its main entrance to Broad Street.

# Martyrs' Memorial

Standing at the south end of St Giles since it was completed in 1843, the Martyrs' Memorial was designed by Sir George Gilbert Scott. The stone monument commemorates the 16th-century Oxford Martyrs. The Oxford Martyrs were tried for heresy in 1555 and, as a result, burnt at the stake for their religious beliefs and teachings. The three martyrs, mentioned earlier in the book, were tried at St Mary the Virgin and were Hugh Latimer, Nicholas Ridley and Archbishop Thomas Cranmer. It is also claimed that these events inspired the nursery rhyme *Three Blind Mice*.